These are Not Poems

BY

Marion TD Lewis

Published by Waterfall Press, Inc. New York, New York

Library of Congress Cataloguing in Publication Data:
Lewis, M
ISBN:0966389344
1. Poetry

Printed in the United States of America
10 9 8 7 6 5 4 3 2 1

To My Ancestors

Table of Contents

Umbrella

The green leaf is wet

because the rain hit it

It sparkles and it drips

And it cleans itself

I am wet

I had to run to get in from the rain

Because I took the risk

that it would not rain

And I did not have

an umbrella

Earth

Earth

lowest point in the universe

Ground zero

How do I know?

Because all roads lead to up from here

How do I know?

Because from the moon we look down

From mars we look down

All the rockets look *down* to the earth

Earth

big bang theory? a bunch of crap

How do I know?

Because big bangs do not result in order

Think about it:

Nagasaki, Hiroshima, World Trade Center, migrants off the coast of Italy

Volcanos, Plane Crashes, tornadoes and tsunamis

All these are big bangs

What we have here is not a big bang

Illogical, inconsistent, ridiculous theory

Wrong theory.

Earth

Sunshine and rain. On cue.

Streams, ponds, oceans and mountains

Fish, tigers, cats, rabbits and zebras

The right pressure to the air

The right distance from the moon and sun

Oxygen, carbon dioxide, sand,

Olive trees, mangos, pure flowing drinking fountains

everything in twos

everything with its opposite

male, female, big, small, hot, cold, sweet, sour, light, dark, hen and cock bees, butterflies and birds

This is a "big bang"?

How come nowhere else got banged up like this?

Earth

round, swirling and circling

Covered in water that stays put

Mountains, deserts, oxygen, food

People hanging upside down down under stay put!

Gravity?

The sky is the floor of this planet

The sky is the ceiling of this planet

Gravity?

Earth

Dirt full of diamonds, rubies, potatoes, onions and oil for us to reap as we sow

A sun that provides essential life; a moon that provides essential light

Just two convenient masses from a big bang? Yea, sure.

Empty underneath (Nothing is under the earth!)

Nothing except for air and wind!

no hell below!

Only infinite heavens above

This is a big bang?

THIS. IS. NOT. A. BIG. BANG.

But is earth hell?

Barking dogs

Bark you not at dogs

For they have vicious molars

With which to tear your flesh

Instead, allow dogs who bark to pass by

And let sleeping dogs continue to sleep

Sounds

NASA says that the sound of the earth

Is the sound of the birds chirping

The sound of the planets

Do not sound like the earth

They sound like the ancient Hindu chakra chants

The sound of the sun is haunting

You can talk to it

It can heal you in fact...

If you talk to it

Wait, that was a plane.

Maybe NASA made a mistake

A bowl of Cereal

I don't give a shit

I don't give a shit

I don't give a shit

Aaargh!

Aaargh!

Aaargh!

But guess what?

What?

It's all your fault!

My fault? How is this my fault?

Problems, problems, always with the problems.

You can't live without problems.

You are not happy without problems.

What do you want me to do?

I can't get out of bed

What do you want *me* to do about that?

Help me!

But you don't give a shit

I am trying!

Fight. Fight little warrior.

Fight yourself, your enemy.

I don't give a shit!

I don't give a shit!

Give a shit.

Give a shit.

No!

Yes!

Okay that's it. Get up. Get the fuck up.

What is your problem? What is wrong with you?

About a half hour ago

I had a bowl of

Cereal

Casablanca

Running as I was to far off places

Casablanca, Dar Es Salaam, Nairobi

Lost among the kiosks and makeshift markets

In dusty towns

Pungent smells of spices and peppers, desert dust and polluted streams

Rice and dried seeds spilling into the dirt

Years after in Johannesburg a man was shot two feet away

Then I returned home via three different boats through four different oceans*

Only to find you were no longer waiting there

Under the olive tree we planted on our first day

As man and wife

You had another man who had taken my bed.

Chip from a Star

Chip from a star

Distant & hot

Giant, bright, light, falling

It is we

LOVE

The opposite of love

Is just a fierce anthropological memory

Shackles from the past

older than Moses

older than time immemorial

older than consciousness

deserving of understanding

deserving of compassion

because it is a disease that comes from a memory

of great hurt that needs to be

soothed, held, hugged, forgiven, understood

The opposite of love

is washed away

only with the expression of love

repeated and multiplied

but be careful

17

it can kill you

You are eternal

You are eternal

a source of a loving universe that has always existed

you have infinite energy and possibility

you are a source of divine love and power

You are eternal

A sublime being that is part of this universe

You can prosper and achieve the greatest possibilities

You are a creature of a magnificent light source

You are eternal

a being integral to the functioning of this world

you breathe and life sources tick and live and produce

You are a being of unlimited & abundant flows of energy

You are eternal

A lavish manifestation of the force that is nature

You forever worthy and deserving of blessings

You are an inspiration to humanity

One Trillion years swirling

A trillion years

Swirling

a billion stars, like Identical rice grains

swirling

a big black hole separating you and me

this was our destiny

swirling

needing one trillion years to form

needing one trillion years to grow

our wings so that we can fly back home together

where it ended

a trillion years from now; where we met a trillion year ago

behind the Indonesian mountains

below the South African seas

through the Aspen snows

Arctic bears and dinosaurs

Swirling above, rice grains & honey bees

mocking us, taunting us

you will never make back!

Swirling

Honeysuckle; meadows and music in the Arabian sea

Can you hear the music

Can you taste the mystery brew

Is this you? Is this me? We fulfilled our destiny!

This time we will never lose our way

Swirling

around a trillion suns

Eouououeoueoueoueouoeououeou!

Echoes, echoing

Eouououeoueoueoueouoeououeou!

long distances

worlds far beyond this one

can you hear? Listen.

They send messages that sound vaguely like thunder

Very faint

The ghosts of Greek and roman philosophers

Have found new theories to their old hypotheses

Because they know now. They were wrong

YOU ARE ALREADY DEAD, they opine

Aliveness is really deadness

The wind finds this amusing

Eouououeoueoueoueouoeououeou!

Donald Trump is really Pope John Paul the twenty-fourth it tells
me

We are already dead?

You stole this idea from Eric Kochel, my old friend

He whispered this to me when he died in 2000

Thief.

It is four o'clock in the morning

I am listening to echoes on an electrical apparatus

I am contemplating my mortality

What if I really am immortal?

My mind is dispersed like sauerkraut

What if this is not the first time I have done this?

What if what I think is being alive is really me being already
dead?

It is too early in the morning for answers

Eououoeoueoueoueouoeououeou!

Infinity

Infinity has a lot of light, and a lot of colour

Vivid blues, purples, yellows, whites and blacks

And a lot of dots, a lot of specks of lavender fireflies

Flying Into infinity;

no ending point

Online, offline in chat rooms and messages

Clouds bubble to infinity

The sun & the Tour Eiffel

The sun is magnetic hanging over the Tuileries

Burning through two giant black clouds that surround it like
warring tribes

At Place de la Concorde, near the fountains, I pause.

"Bonjour," I say to the bright spot half the size of my handbag,
in the far distance

Bright and hot it burns my skin in spite of the cover of clouds

It seeks me out, identifies me by name,

answers my salutation with a diamond shaped wink

For two years it has done this every single day

since that day when I said "I *see* you."

It is as if it is saying "No, I see YOU!"

one day it flung itself against the side of the Tour Montparnasse

at a very strange hour while I was teaching a little boy who lived
near the Bon Marché

I was astonished and awe-struck "This thing is aggressive," I
thought

Every day, like today, it finds me and makes it impossible for me
to ignore it

It pulls my gaze and my attention, like a magnet

To my right, the Tour Eiffel resplendent and glorious

tries fruitlessly to compete for my attention

Night falls

Night falls

Pigeons close their eyes

daisies close their petals

The sun disappears

The children hide their faces

While my heart races

The sky is moonless tonight

The boxer is ready to fight

Maybe I should put the daisies

back into the pretty white vases...

Life

The beauty of the earth flummoxes me

How perfectly put together is everything I see

Its awesomeness and wonder astonishes me

How clear it is that this is the work of an artist and designer

A chef & lover of carnal pleasures, humour, love

a specimen with perfect vision, scale and proportion

the ultimate creator

The notion that the earth created itself? insane

But who did it and why?

Who created this thing?

Did who did it disappear in the doing?

Did who did it self-destruct?

If not, where is who did it hiding?

Is who did it under the couch?

Is who did it sitting in my living room?

29

Is who did it sunbathing on a cloud?

I can't believe this

Can you believe this?

Do you see what I see?

Do you hear what I hear?

How is this happenstance?

How can this be a big bang?

There is something we don't understand.

There is a missing piece

"Life" is a mystery

Given to humanity like a bank loan

We have to pay it back

We have to give it back with interest

Are we going to default?

Think of a world without borders

Migrants on their way to Italy

Drowning in a capsized boat, dead

Syria

Mexico

Africa

Poland

People desperate, moving from one corner to the next

A humanitarian crisis says Ban Ki Moon

A little dead boy washed up on the beach

I can't look

Who made these lines in the desert sands?

Who created these invisible Berlin walls

That lock people out?

It was meant to be this way, pop says

Because people are different

They look different

They belong in different parts

Is that so, pop?

I am not sure

Where do we go from here?

I don't know but I tell you what: Don't dilly dally

Does God ever take a bathroom break?

Does god just sit there on a throne all day long for millennia listening to cherubim sing?

Or does he get up sometimes to go for a jog?

Does he eat breakfast?

Does he go to the bathroom?

Dear God, I love you; you fascinate me

I want to ask you some questions

Is this OK?

I want to know if you are my father or my uncle?

Can I call you Uncle God instead of Father?

I think you are my uncle because my father would have spoiled me more

Dear God I want to know if all this was an explosion?

Can you answer me that? The scientists say it was

Dear God I want to know if we are already dead?

Is this a crazy idea that my friend Eric whispered to me when he died?

Dear God I want to know how come all roads lead to up from the Earth?

Is Earth hell?

Dear God I want to know why you put us down here?

Was it to banish us and to damn us for past wrongs?

Or is it a second chance?

Is life a second chance, God?

Do you expect us to stay here and make amends?

I love you God but I don't understand you.

What was your strategy and objective

When you did all this?

And where are you now?

What are you doing?

Are you having coffee?

Do you have a wife?

Are you exhausted?

Blue fire

A blue fire rages in my heart

A fire so strong and destructive

it could cause the entire state of California to combust

A fire so hot and destructive

It could melt massive plates of titanium

A fire so hot and destructive

In Fahrenheit is compares to the surface of the sun

This tsunami of emotion

Bubbles to the edge of my lips

Turning my tongue to molten lava

If I dare open my mouth

Babylon itself will eject from my jaws

So I use my teeth to hold my tongue

in a vicelike grip

Intuition

Intuition is memory

Of something past that really happened

Although "past" is a misleading idea

Since there is no past only a

Transparent timeless bubble

That encapsulates all galaxies

And keeps everything turning

In a circular fashion, eternally

With a strange precision

How can I access my intuition

In a way that resolves all questions about

Who I am in juxtaposition to

All others?

Because only with intuition will I be able

to fully understand this experience

and only then will I finally be able to

understand this thing called my life

A strange mathematical theorem

That defies my greatest Pythagorean efforts

To prove.

O beautiful Queen

Her steadfast gaze and poise

Her silent voice an otherworldly noise

Her voice casting a hypnotic spell

Into my subconscious well

Quiet and serene

She sits resplendent on her throne

With regal posture & a savory

Jazmin and raspberry odor

Humble being without a dime

Had I lived in her time

I never could have entered her court

Though perhaps I could have witnessed her *mort*

Her annus horribilis

a bad year indeed it was

She lost her beautiful head

In a guillotine prepared by an angry mob

Now she sits in my salon astride my easel

Bedecked in beautiful vivid primary red and gold

Her haunting eyes, unforgettable

And her Mona Lisa smile unperturbed.

The great light

There is a great Light

A great light that is genesis

A great light that is Exodus, Leviticus and Numbers

A great light of supreme love

A great light of super-human power

A great light of total acceptance

No exclusions – TOTAL ACCEPTANCE

All beings are part of this light

All beings are enveloped by this light

All beings are watched by this light

All beings are expected by this light

All beings are awaited at the gateway by this light

The guy sitting homelessly in the

Metro Pasteur in the 15th arrondissement is equally awaited

As the woman next to him in her freshly

showered skin and well-oiled hair

God is that light; God is *the* light

The definite and indefinite light; perfect light(s)

Singular and plural light(s)

visible and invisible light(s)

A field magnetic of light(s)

A ray, many rays of light(s)

Coloured lights, uncoloured lights,

Magic lights, miracle lights

lights of infinite power and possibility

steadfast unebbing light(s)

Many-colored light, one-coloured light(s)

The rainbow hints of the wondrous light(s)

Sparkling and reverberating lights (s)

Tibetan beats remind me of them

41

Quantum leap

I must take a quantum leap into the celestial capsule

Me, sole voyager swimming in celestial oceans

Of white lights and black lights, green lights and blue lights

My greatest fear among many great fears

Is that when I reach my destination

I will not find Jerusalem

<u>Me</u>

Thankfully

I have

Me

I am here

When things

Are great

And not so

Great

All the time

I give my

Shadow

A guide

Dear Reader,

I hope you enjoyed my "poems." I wish you a life full of abundance and love and consciousness. By the latter I mean an awareness that there exists a power that is greater than us. It really does exist – whatever you choose to call it. And I do not mean this in a religious sense. You do not have to subscribe to a religion to become conscious that something else is there. And it is a pretty amazing, beautiful and loving something that gave you the gift of yourself. And remember that you - both individually and collectively - are capable of very good, powerful and transformative things.

Thanks for Reading! Best Wishes!

Marion

www.ingramcontent.com/pod-product-compliance
Lightning Source LLC
Chambersburg PA
CBHW060630030426
42337CB00018B/3285